PRINCEWILL LAGANG

Marriage Made in Heaven: A Christian Guide to Love

First published by PRINCEWILL LAGANG 2023

Copyright © 2023 by Princewill Lagang

All rights reserved. No part of this publication may be reproduced, stored or transmitted in any form or by any means, electronic, mechanical, photocopying, recording, scanning, or otherwise without written permission from the publisher. It is illegal to copy this book, post it to a website, or distribute it by any other means without permission.

Princewill Lagang asserts the moral right to be identified as the author of this work.

First edition

This book was professionally typeset on Reedsy. Find out more at reedsy.com

Contents

1	The Divine Blueprint	1
2	The Foundation of Love: Faith and Relationship with God	4
3	The Power of Graceful Communication	7
4	Intimacy in Christian Marriage	10
5	Navigating Challenges and Adversity with Faith	13
6	Sharing Goals and Dreams	16
7	The Heart of Servanthood	19
8	The Healing Power of Forgiveness	22
9	Leaving a Legacy of Love and Faith	25
10	Reflecting on a Journey of Love and Faith	28
11	Nurturing Everlasting Love	31
12	Looking Ahead with Hope	34

1

The Divine Blueprint

In the Beginning…

In the beginning, before the foundations of the world were laid, there was love. Love was the very essence of the divine, flowing from the heart of God Himself. It was this love that set the stage for the greatest love story ever told—the story of God's love for humanity, a love so deep and profound that it transcends time and space. This love story is the foundation upon which every human love story is built.

As Christians, we are called to love as God loves. In the pages of this book, we will explore the beautiful journey of love and marriage, guided by the principles of the Christian faith. Our goal is to provide a comprehensive guide for individuals seeking to build and sustain marriages that reflect the love and grace of God.

The Divine Design

God's design for love and marriage is evident from the very beginning of the

Bible. In the book of Genesis, we read about the creation of the first man, Adam. God, in His infinite wisdom, saw that it was not good for Adam to be alone and said, "It is not good that the man should be alone; I will make him a helper fit for him" (Genesis 2:18, ESV). God created Eve, the first woman, from Adam's rib, and thus, the first marriage was established.

This divine act of creating woman from man's rib carries profound symbolism. It signifies that in marriage, man and woman are meant to be equal partners, each complementing the other. They are not identical, but they are uniquely suited to fit together. This initial union is a clear reflection of the complementary nature of marriage as designed by God.

The Marriage Covenant

Marriage, as ordained by God, is not a mere social contract or a romantic partnership but a sacred covenant. This covenantal aspect is what sets Christian marriage apart from secular unions. In a covenant, two individuals commit themselves to each other in the presence of God, with a solemn promise to love, honor, and cherish one another, no matter what challenges may come their way.

This commitment mirrors the covenant between God and His people. Throughout the Bible, we see references to the marriage-like relationship between God and His people, particularly in the Old Testament. God's unfailing love and His people's faithfulness (or lack thereof) provide a powerful metaphor for the love and commitment within a Christian marriage.

Love That Reflects God's Love

Christian love is not mere infatuation, and Christian marriage is not just a human institution. It's a reflection of God's love for us. "We love because he first loved us" (1 John 4:19, ESV). Our love for our spouses should mirror God's love for His children, selfless, sacrificial, and unconditional.

In the subsequent chapters of this book, we will delve into the practical aspects of how to build and nurture a Christian marriage. We will explore topics such as communication, intimacy, conflict resolution, and spiritual growth as they relate to the marriage journey.

Our hope is that by the end of this book, you will be better equipped to embark on or enhance your own "Marriage Made in Heaven," where your love story becomes a testament to the divine love story that began with God's love for His people.

In Conclusion

The blueprint for Christian love and marriage is laid out for us in the Bible. In the pages that follow, we will delve into the details of how to build a love that reflects God's love, how to nurture a marriage that honors the divine covenant, and how to create a bond that withstands the tests of time. It's a journey worth taking, for in the pursuit of a "Marriage Made in Heaven," we come closer to understanding the very heart of God.

As we begin this journey, let us remember the words of 1 Corinthians 13:4-7 (ESV), "Love is patient and kind; love does not envy or boast; it is not arrogant or rude. It does not insist on its own way; it is not irritable or resentful; it does not rejoice at wrongdoing, but rejoices with the truth. Love bears all things, believes all things, hopes all things, endures all things."

With these words as our guide, let us embark on the beautiful adventure of Christian love and marriage.

2

The Foundation of Love: Faith and Relationship with God

Faith, Love, and Unity

In the previous chapter, we established that Christian love and marriage are built upon the divine blueprint, reflecting God's love and the covenant between Him and His people. But how do we make this blueprint a reality in our own lives? The answer lies in the foundation of love: faith and a deep relationship with God.

A Relationship with the Divine

In the Christian tradition, we believe that God is love (1 John 4:8, ESV), and He is the source of all love. Thus, building a loving and lasting marriage begins with fostering a personal relationship with God. By seeking Him in our lives and striving to know Him intimately, we can tap into the wellspring of divine love.

THE FOUNDATION OF LOVE: FAITH AND RELATIONSHIP WITH GOD

Faith as the Cornerstone

Faith is the cornerstone of a Christian marriage. It is the bedrock upon which love and commitment are built. Faith is not just a set of religious beliefs but a trust and confidence in God's plan for our lives. In the context of marriage, faith means trusting that God has brought you together for a purpose, even when challenges arise.

The Threefold Cord

In Ecclesiastes 4:12 (ESV), it is written, "And though a man might prevail against one who is alone, two will withstand him—a threefold cord is not quickly broken." In the context of marriage, this passage emphasizes the importance of including God as the third cord that binds husband and wife together.

When we invite God into our marriage, we strengthen the relationship and provide a solid foundation for love to grow. God's presence is like a guiding light that helps couples navigate the storms of life and find their way back to love and unity.

Practical Steps for Building Faith

- Prayer: Regular, heartfelt prayers as a couple and individually will strengthen your connection with God. It allows you to share your concerns, joys, and desires with Him.

- Bible Study: Spending time in the Word of God deepens your understanding of His love and purpose for marriage. You can study together, discuss passages, and apply the teachings to your relationship.

- Worship: Attending church services and engaging in acts of worship as a couple reinforces your faith and sense of belonging to a larger Christian community.

- Seeking Spiritual Guidance: Don't hesitate to seek guidance from pastors, mentors, or Christian counselors when facing difficulties. They can provide valuable insights and support in aligning your marriage with God's plan.

Unity in Diversity

In a Christian marriage, faith and love bring unity out of diversity. Husbands and wives often have differing personalities, backgrounds, and perspectives. However, the shared faith in God and love for one another create a harmonious bond that transcends these differences.

In Conclusion

A Christian marriage, like any strong building, requires a solid foundation. The foundation is your faith and relationship with God. When you seek God together, rely on Him, and make Him the center of your marriage, you create a strong, unbreakable base for your love. In the chapters to come, we will explore how this foundation of faith can shape your communication, intimacy, and overall journey in building a marriage made in heaven.

Remember the words of Proverbs 24:3-4 (ESV): "By wisdom a house is built, and by understanding it is established; by knowledge the rooms are filled with all precious and pleasant riches." Building a house of love with God as its foundation is an endeavor filled with precious and pleasant riches, and it's a journey worth taking.

In Chapter 3, we will delve into the essential element of communication in a Christian marriage.

3

The Power of Graceful Communication

The Art of Listening and Speaking

Communication is the heartbeat of any relationship, and in a Christian marriage, it is the means by which love and understanding are shared. In this chapter, we will explore the power of graceful communication as a vital tool for nurturing and strengthening your "Marriage Made in Heaven."

Communication as a Divine Gift

In 1 Peter 4:11 (ESV), we read, "Whoever speaks, as one who speaks oracles of God; whoever serves, as one who serves by the strength that God supplies." Communication is a divine gift, and when we use it wisely, we honor God's intention for our relationships.

The Language of Love

Love speaks a language of its own, and it's often conveyed through words, tone, and body language. In a Christian marriage, the words we choose and the way we express them are critical. Ephesians 4:29 (ESV) reminds us, "Let no corrupting talk come out of your mouths, but only such as is good for building up, as fits the occasion, that it may give grace to those who hear." Our words should bring grace and edification, not harm.

The Power of Listening

Effective communication is a two-way street. In James 1:19 (ESV), it is written, "Know this, my beloved brothers: let every person be quick to hear, slow to speak, slow to anger." Listening is an essential aspect of communication, and it involves being fully present and attentive to your spouse's thoughts, feelings, and concerns.

Conflict Resolution and Forgiveness

Conflicts are an inevitable part of any relationship. In a Christian marriage, we are called to address these conflicts with love, grace, and a spirit of reconciliation. Matthew 18:15 (ESV) provides guidance: "If your brother sins against you, go and tell him his fault, between you and him alone. If he listens to you, you have gained your brother." This principle can be applied within marriage.

Forgiveness, too, is a central component of graceful communication. As Christians, we are called to forgive as we have been forgiven by God. Ephesians 4:32 (ESV) instructs us to "be kind to one another, tenderhearted, forgiving one another, as God in Christ forgave you."

Practical Tips for Graceful Communication

1. Open and Honest Dialog: Encourage open and honest communication in your marriage. Create a safe space for your spouse to express their thoughts and feelings without fear of judgment.

2. Choose Your Words Carefully: Be mindful of the words you use and their impact. Words can build up or tear down; choose to build.

3. Active Listening: Practice active listening by fully focusing on your spouse when they speak, without interrupting or formulating your response in advance.

4. Conflict Resolution: Approach conflicts with a solution-oriented mindset and a commitment to reconciliation.

5. Forgiveness: Forgive and seek forgiveness genuinely. Remember that grace is at the heart of a Christian marriage.

In Conclusion

Effective communication is a fundamental building block of a "Marriage Made in Heaven." By mastering the art of graceful communication, you create a space where love can flourish, conflicts can be resolved, and forgiveness can be freely given. In the next chapter, we will explore the importance of intimacy and how it deepens the bond between spouses in a Christian marriage.

As we continue on this journey toward a love that reflects God's love, let us remember the wisdom of Proverbs 18:21 (ESV): "Death and life are in the power of the tongue." Choose life. Choose love. Choose grace in your communication.

4

Intimacy in Christian Marriage

Deepening the Connection

Intimacy in a Christian marriage goes beyond physical closeness; it encompasses emotional, spiritual, and physical connections that strengthen the bond between spouses. In this chapter, we will explore the multifaceted nature of intimacy and how it deepens your "Marriage Made in Heaven."

Understanding Intimacy

In Song of Solomon 7:10 (ESV), we find the words, "I am my beloved's, and his desire is for me." This verse encapsulates the essence of marital intimacy. Intimacy is the recognition that you belong to each other, and it involves a deep, mutual desire for closeness.

Emotional Intimacy

Emotional intimacy is built on trust and vulnerability. It is the willingness to share your deepest thoughts, fears, and dreams with your spouse. Proverbs

27:9 (ESV) beautifully describes it: "Oil and perfume make the heart glad, and the sweetness of a friend comes from his earnest counsel." Your spouse should be your closest and most trusted friend.

Spiritual Intimacy

The foundation of spiritual intimacy is your shared faith and the journey you take together in your relationship with God. When you pray, worship, and study the Bible together, you strengthen your spiritual connection. Ecclesiastes 4:12 (ESV) reminds us of the power of unity in a spiritual context, "And though a man might prevail against one who is alone, two will withstand him—a threefold cord is not quickly broken."

Physical Intimacy

Physical intimacy is an essential aspect of marriage, and it's a beautiful expression of love. It's not only about the act of physical closeness but also the affection, tenderness, and respect that you show to each other. 1 Corinthians 7:3-4 (ESV) emphasizes the importance of physical intimacy within marriage: "The husband should give to his wife her conjugal rights, and likewise the wife to her husband. For the wife does not have authority over her own body, but the husband does. Likewise, the husband does not have authority over his own body, but the wife does."

Practical Steps to Enhance Intimacy

1. Open and Honest Communication: Share your thoughts, desires, and concerns related to intimacy. Discuss what makes you both feel loved and cherished.

2. Prioritize Quality Time: Spend quality time together without distractions. Date nights and special moments can rekindle the emotional and physical aspects of your relationship.

3. Spiritual Connection: Attend church services, pray, and read the Bible together to nurture your spiritual bond.

4. Learn Each Other's Love Languages: Understand your spouse's love language and express your love in ways that resonate with them.

5. Seek Professional Help if Needed: If you encounter difficulties related to intimacy, don't hesitate to seek guidance from a Christian counselor or therapist.

In Conclusion

Intimacy in a Christian marriage is a journey of deepening connection. It's about recognizing the beauty of emotional, spiritual, and physical closeness and valuing your spouse as your beloved. As you continue to cultivate intimacy, you're drawing closer to the ideal "Marriage Made in Heaven."

In Chapter 5, we will explore the role of faith in facing challenges and adversity within your marriage, recognizing that even in trials, God's grace prevails.

Remember the wisdom of 1 Peter 3:7 (ESV): "Likewise, husbands, live with your wives in an understanding way, showing honor to the woman as the weaker vessel, since they are heirs with you of the grace of life, so that your prayers may not be hindered."

5

Navigating Challenges and Adversity with Faith

Drawing Closer in Difficult Times

In every marriage, there come moments of trial and adversity. How you and your spouse face these challenges can greatly impact the strength and longevity of your relationship. This chapter explores how faith and trust in God can be a guiding light during such times and how they can help you draw closer to each other.

Challenges in Marriage

Marriage is a journey with its share of ups and downs. Challenges can come in various forms, such as financial difficulties, health issues, conflicts, and external stressors. What sets Christian marriages apart is the belief that God is present in the midst of these challenges.

The Role of Faith in Challenges

In times of trouble, faith in God becomes the anchor that holds your marriage steady. Psalm 46:1 (ESV) assures us, "God is our refuge and strength, a very present help in trouble." Knowing that God is with you as a couple, supporting and guiding you through difficulties, provides strength and comfort.

Trusting God's Plan

In Proverbs 3:5-6 (ESV), we are encouraged to "Trust in the Lord with all your heart and do not lean on your own understanding. In all your ways acknowledge him, and he will make straight your paths." Trusting in God's plan, even when it doesn't align with your own, can be challenging, but it's a crucial aspect of facing adversity with faith.

Drawing Closer in Trials

Challenges can either drive a couple apart or bring them closer together. In a Christian marriage, adversity offers an opportunity to strengthen your bond. As you face trials hand in hand, supporting and praying for each other, your love and connection deepen.

Practical Steps in Facing Challenges

1. Prayer: Pray together and individually for strength, guidance, and solutions to the challenges you're facing.

2. Seeking Support: Don't hesitate to seek support from your church community, mentors, or counselors. They can provide valuable advice and encouragement.

3. Maintaining Open Communication: Continue to communicate openly and honestly, sharing your fears, concerns, and hopes with each other.

4. Focus on Gratitude: Amid challenges, practice gratitude for the positive

aspects of your relationship and the support you provide each other.

5. Resilience and Patience: Remember that challenges are temporary, and with faith and patience, you can overcome them.

In Conclusion

Adversity is an inevitable part of life and, consequently, of marriage. However, in a Christian marriage, challenges are not obstacles but opportunities to demonstrate faith and love. By drawing closer to God and each other during difficult times, you can reinforce your commitment to the ideal "Marriage Made in Heaven."

In Chapter 6, we will explore the importance of shared goals and dreams in a Christian marriage and how they can strengthen your unity and love.

As you continue your journey of love, remember the words of Romans 12:12 (ESV): "Rejoice in hope, be patient in tribulation, be constant in prayer." These principles can guide you through any adversity you encounter.

6

Sharing Goals and Dreams

Building a Future Together

A Christian marriage is not just about the present; it's also about the future. In this chapter, we will explore the significance of shared goals and dreams within your marriage and how they can strengthen your unity and love.

The Power of Shared Vision

Proverbs 29:18 (ESV) reminds us that "Where there is no prophetic vision the people cast off restraint, but blessed is he who keeps the law." A shared vision for your marriage gives direction and purpose. It's the compass that guides you through life's journey together.

Defining Your Shared Goals

Begin by defining your shared goals and dreams. These could be related to your faith, family, career, or other areas of life. Consider questions like:

- What do we hope to achieve together in our faith journey?
    - How do we envision our family life in the coming years?
    - Where do we want to be professionally or personally?

Embracing Flexibility

While shared goals are important, it's also crucial to remain flexible. Life is filled with unexpected twists and turns, and it's important to adapt to changes while keeping your shared vision in mind. Proverbs 19:21 (ESV) teaches us that "Many are the plans in the mind of a man, but it is the purpose of the Lord that will stand."

Encouraging Individual Growth

Supporting each other's individual growth and aspirations is also vital. Proverbs 20:5 (ESV) reminds us that "The purpose in a man's heart is like deep water, but a man of understanding will draw it out." In a Christian marriage, understanding each other's dreams and helping one another achieve them is a sign of love and support.

Practical Steps in Sharing Goals and Dreams

1. Communication: Regularly discuss your aspirations and the future you envision as a couple. Listen to your spouse's dreams and share your own.

2. Set Short- and Long-Term Goals: Create a list of short-term and long-term goals together. This can include personal, professional, and spiritual aspirations.

3. Pray Together: Praying together for your shared goals and dreams can strengthen your faith and unity.

4. Review and Adjust: Periodically review your goals, adjust them as needed,

and celebrate your achievements together.

5. Celebrate Milestones: Celebrate your successes along the way, both big and small. This will motivate and encourage you to keep pursuing your shared vision.

In Conclusion

A Christian marriage is a partnership in which you build your future together with faith, love, and a shared vision. By defining and pursuing shared goals and dreams, you're creating a roadmap for your journey toward the ideal "Marriage Made in Heaven."

In Chapter 7, we will explore the concept of servanthood in Christian marriage, emphasizing the importance of selflessness, humility, and mutual support.

Remember the wisdom of Proverbs 16:3 (ESV): "Commit your work to the Lord, and your plans will be established." When you commit your marriage and its dreams to the Lord, your path becomes clearer.

7

The Heart of Servanthood

The Beauty of Selflessness and Mutual Support

In this chapter, we will delve into the concept of servanthood within a Christian marriage. The heart of servanthood lies in selflessness, humility, and mutual support. Understanding and practicing this principle can profoundly impact your "Marriage Made in Heaven."

The Example of Christ

The foundation of servanthood within Christian marriage is modeled after the life and teachings of Jesus Christ. In Mark 10:45 (ESV), He says, "For even the Son of Man came not to be served but to serve, and to give his life as a ransom for many." As Christians, we are called to emulate His selfless and sacrificial love.

Selflessness and Sacrifice

Servanthood in marriage involves putting your spouse's needs before your own. Philippians 2:3-4 (ESV) instructs, "Do nothing from rivalry or conceit, but in humility count others more significant than yourselves. Let each of you look not only to his own interests, but also to the interests of others." This selflessness creates an atmosphere of love and support within the marriage.

Mutual Support

In a Christian marriage, servanthood is a two-way street. It means supporting and encouraging each other in your individual endeavors and dreams. Galatians 6:2 (ESV) reinforces this idea: "Bear one another's burdens, and so fulfill the law of Christ."

Practical Steps Toward Servanthood

1. Acts of Kindness: Practice small, daily acts of kindness to show your love and support for your spouse.

2. Open Communication: Be attentive to your spouse's needs and concerns. Listen actively and respond with empathy.

3. Mutual Decision-Making: Include your spouse in important decisions, respecting their perspective and desires.

4. Encourage Individual Growth: Support your spouse's personal and professional growth, and celebrate their achievements.

5. Shared Responsibilities: Share the responsibilities in your home and family life, working together as a team.

In Conclusion

The heart of servanthood is the embodiment of love and mutual support within a Christian marriage. It reflects the selflessness and humility taught by Jesus and creates a strong foundation for a "Marriage Made in Heaven."

In Chapter 8, we will explore the importance of forgiveness and reconciliation within a Christian marriage, highlighting how these practices can heal wounds and strengthen your bond.

Remember the words of 1 Peter 4:10 (ESV): "As each has received a gift, use it to serve one another, as good stewards of God's varied grace." By serving one another in love, you become good stewards of the grace that binds your marriage.

8

The Healing Power of Forgiveness

Restoring Harmony and Strength

Forgiveness is a fundamental aspect of a Christian marriage. It is the key to healing wounds, reconciling differences, and strengthening your bond. In this chapter, we will explore the importance of forgiveness and reconciliation within your "Marriage Made in Heaven."

The Call to Forgive

Forgiveness is at the core of Christian faith. In Ephesians 4:32 (ESV), we are reminded, "Be kind to one another, tenderhearted, forgiving one another, as God in Christ forgave you." Just as God forgives us for our shortcomings and sins, we are called to extend the same grace to our spouses.

Healing and Restoration

In every marriage, there will be moments of hurt, misunderstanding, and conflict. These experiences can create wounds in the relationship. Forgiveness is the healing balm that restores harmony and strengthens the marriage.

It allows you to move forward with a renewed sense of love and unity.

Reconciliation

Forgiveness and reconciliation go hand in hand. While forgiveness is about releasing grudges and offering grace, reconciliation involves rebuilding trust and restoring the bond between spouses. 2 Corinthians 5:18 (ESV) encourages us, "All this is from God, who through Christ reconciled us to himself and gave us the ministry of reconciliation."

Practical Steps to Forgive and Reconcile

1. Acknowledge the Hurt: Recognize the pain and hurt caused by conflicts or mistakes within the marriage.

2. Pray for Guidance: Seek guidance and strength from God through prayer to help you forgive and reconcile.

3. Talk Openly: Engage in open and honest communication with your spouse. Share your feelings and concerns, and listen to theirs as well.

4. Offer and Accept Forgiveness: Extend forgiveness and grace, and be willing to accept forgiveness when it's offered to you.

5. Rebuild Trust: Work together to rebuild trust and restore the intimacy and connection in your relationship.

In Conclusion

Forgiveness and reconciliation are essential to the longevity and health of your Christian marriage. By forgiving and reconciling with your spouse, you create a space where love and unity can flourish. It is through these acts of grace that you come closer to the ideal "Marriage Made in Heaven."

In Chapter 9, we will explore the legacy of love and faith that you can leave for future generations. Your marriage has the power to inspire and guide those who come after you.

Remember the wisdom of Colossians 3:13 (ESV): "Bearing with one another and, if one has a complaint against another, forgiving each other; as the Lord has forgiven you, so you also must forgive." By forgiving as the Lord forgives, you honor His love in your marriage.

9

Leaving a Legacy of Love and Faith

Inspiring Generations with Your Marriage

Your Christian marriage is more than just a union between two people; it is a testament to the love and faith that can inspire generations. In this chapter, we will explore how your marriage can leave a lasting legacy of love, faith, and hope for those who come after you.

The Impact of a Godly Marriage

A marriage built on love and faith is a powerful witness to the world. It reflects the divine love story between God and His people, and it has the potential to impact not only your immediate family but also your community and future generations.

Guiding Principles for Leaving a Legacy

To leave a legacy of love and faith, consider these guiding principles:

1. Modeling Love: Your marriage should serve as a model of love, respect,

and selflessness. Ephesians 5:25 (ESV) states, "Husbands, love your wives, as Christ loved the church and gave himself up for her." This sacrificial love sets an example for others.

2. Passing on Faith: Share your faith with your children and those around you. Deuteronomy 6:5-7 (ESV) encourages parents to teach their children diligently, "You shall love the Lord your God with all your heart and with all your soul and with all your might. And these words that I command you today shall be on your heart. You shall teach them diligently to your children."

3. Supporting Others: Extend support, guidance, and encouragement to those seeking to build strong, faith-based marriages. Offer mentorship and share your experiences to inspire others.

4. Investing in Your Community: Be actively involved in your church and community. Your strong and loving marriage can be a source of encouragement and hope to those who may be struggling.

Practical Steps to Leave a Legacy

1. Teach by Example: Live out the principles of love, faith, and respect in your daily life.

2. Share Your Story: Share your journey as a couple, including the challenges you've overcome and the lessons you've learned.

3. Pass on Traditions: Establish family traditions that promote faith, unity, and love. This could include prayer, worship, or acts of service.

4. Be a Mentor: Offer guidance and support to younger couples seeking to build their own strong marriages.

5. Involve the Next Generation: Involve your children in activities that

nurture their faith and understanding of love within the family.

In Conclusion

Your marriage is a story of love, faith, and hope that can transcend your lifetime. By actively seeking to leave a legacy of love and faith, you honor the divine plan for marriage and become a source of inspiration for future generations.

In the final chapter, we will reflect on the journey we've taken together, reaffirming the beauty of a "Marriage Made in Heaven" and the eternal significance of a loving and faith-filled relationship.

Remember the words of 1 Corinthians 16:14 (ESV): "Let all that you do be done in love." By living your marriage with love and faith, you fulfill this calling and leave a powerful legacy.

10

Reflecting on a Journey of Love and Faith

The Beauty and Eternal Significance of a "Marriage Made in Heaven"

As we reach the final chapter of this book, it's time to reflect on the journey we've taken together and the enduring significance of a Christian marriage built on love and faith.

The Divine Blueprint of Love

Throughout this book, we've explored the concept of a "Marriage Made in Heaven" as a reflection of the divine blueprint for love. We've seen how faith, communication, intimacy, shared goals, servanthood, forgiveness, and leaving a legacy of love and faith are all integral parts of this divine plan.

The Eternal Significance

A Christian marriage is more than a worldly contract; it is a sacred covenant. It's a reflection of God's love and a glimpse into the eternal love story between Christ and His Church. In Ephesians 5:31-32 (ESV), we read, "Therefore a man shall leave his father and mother and hold fast to his wife, and the two shall become one flesh. This mystery is profound, and I am saying that it refers to Christ and the church." Your love story, too, is part of this profound mystery.

A Love That Endures

In 1 Corinthians 13:13 (ESV), we are reminded, "So now faith, hope, and love abide, these three; but the greatest of these is love." Love, as we've explored throughout this book, is the cornerstone of a Christian marriage. It's a love that endures through the trials and joys of life, reflecting the enduring love of Christ.

Cherishing Your "Marriage Made in Heaven"

As you reflect on your own "Marriage Made in Heaven," consider the following:

- What have been the most significant lessons you've learned on this journey of love and faith?
    - How have you seen your faith and love grow and evolve in your marriage?
    - In what ways has your marriage reflected the divine love story between Christ and His Church?

In Conclusion

A Christian marriage is a journey of love and faith, guided by God's plan. It's a reflection of His love, grace, and eternal purpose. By nurturing and cherishing your "Marriage Made in Heaven," you not only enrich your own lives but also become a source of inspiration to others, leaving a lasting legacy of love and faith.

As you continue to build your "Marriage Made in Heaven," remember the wisdom of 1 Corinthians 16:14 (ESV): "Let all that you do be done in love."

With love as your guiding principle, your marriage is a testament to God's enduring love and a beautiful reflection of the divine love story.

Thank you for joining me on this journey of love and faith within a Christian marriage. May your "Marriage Made in Heaven" continue to be a source of joy, strength, and inspiration for years to come.

11

Nurturing Everlasting Love

Sustaining and Renewing Your "Marriage Made in Heaven"

As you continue your journey of love in your Christian marriage, it's important to nurture and sustain the love you've built. In this chapter, we will explore the practices and principles that can help you maintain and renew the love in your "Marriage Made in Heaven."

The Dynamic Nature of Love

Love within a marriage is dynamic and ever-changing. It requires ongoing care and attention to thrive. In Song of Solomon 8:7 (ESV), we find a beautiful description of love's enduring strength: "Many waters cannot quench love, neither can floods drown it."

Continual Communication

Open and honest communication remains a cornerstone of a strong marriage. Continually discuss your feelings, concerns, and dreams with your spouse. Share your thoughts, hopes, and experiences as you navigate life's journey together.

Quality Time Together

Amid the demands of daily life, it's essential to set aside quality time for each other. Whether it's date nights, weekend getaways, or simply sharing a meal together, these moments strengthen your connection and reignite the flame of love.

Growing Together Spiritually

Nurture your spiritual connection by praying, studying the Bible, and worshiping together. A shared faith can deepen your bond and provide strength and guidance through life's challenges.

Forgiveness and Grace

Continually practice forgiveness and grace in your marriage. As challenges arise, as they inevitably will, the ability to forgive and offer grace is a testament to the enduring nature of love.

Cherishing the Moments

Take time to cherish the special moments in your marriage. Celebrate milestones, anniversaries, and the little victories. Express gratitude for the love and support you've found in each other.

Rekindling the Flame

Sometimes, love may need rekindling. Don't be discouraged by seasons of distance or disconnection. Instead, take steps to rekindle the flame through acts of kindness, physical affection, and intentional time together.

The Importance of Laughter

Laughter is a powerful tool in maintaining love. Enjoy humor and lightheartedness in your relationship. Proverbs 17:22 (ESV) reminds us, "A joyful heart is good medicine, but a crushed spirit dries up the bones."

In Conclusion

A "Marriage Made in Heaven" is not a static entity; it's a living, evolving love story. By continually nurturing and renewing your love, you ensure that it remains a source of joy, strength, and inspiration for both of you.

As you move forward, remember the wisdom of Colossians 3:14 (ESV): "And above all these put on love, which binds everything together in perfect harmony." By putting on love and nurturing it, you maintain the harmony in your marriage and experience the beauty of a love that endures.

12

Looking Ahead with Hope

The Eternal Promise of a "Marriage Made in Heaven"

As we conclude our journey through this guide to love within a Christian marriage, let's reflect on the eternal promise and hope that a "Marriage Made in Heaven" represents. This chapter explores the importance of looking ahead with hope and the lasting impact of your faith-filled love story.

The Eternal Promise

A Christian marriage is rooted in the eternal promise of God's love. It reflects the profound relationship between Christ and His Church, as described in Ephesians 5:31-32 (ESV): "Therefore a man shall leave his father and mother and hold fast to his wife, and the two shall become one flesh. This mystery is profound, and I am saying that it refers to Christ and the church." Your marriage is a glimpse of this divine and eternal love.

A Beacon of Hope

Your "Marriage Made in Heaven" serves as a beacon of hope for a world often filled with chaos and uncertainty. It is a testament to the power of love, faith, and commitment, and it inspires others to seek and nurture similar relationships.

The Legacy of Love

Throughout this journey, we've explored how your marriage can leave a legacy of love and faith. The impact of your love story doesn't end with you; it has the potential to inspire generations to come.

Continuing Growth

A "Marriage Made in Heaven" is a journey of continual growth. As you look ahead, recognize that the love and faith you've cultivated will continue to evolve. Embrace new chapters in your relationship with anticipation and a sense of purpose.

The Role of Faith

Your faith remains a guiding force in your marriage. It is the anchor that keeps you steady in the storms of life. As you look ahead with hope, place your faith in God's plan for your marriage, trusting that He will lead you through each season.

Renewed Commitment

As you conclude this guide, take a moment to renew your commitment to each other. Remember the vows you exchanged and the love that has brought you this far. Look ahead with a sense of purpose and excitement, knowing that your "Marriage Made in Heaven" is a journey of endless love and faith.

In Conclusion

A "Marriage Made in Heaven" is a divine gift. It reflects God's love for His people and holds the promise of an enduring love story. By nurturing your love, faith, and commitment, you not only enrich your own lives but also serve as a testament to the enduring power of love for those who come after you.

As you look ahead with hope, remember the wisdom of Jeremiah 29:11 (ESV): "For I know the plans I have for you, declares the Lord, plans for welfare and not for evil, to give you a future and a hope." May your "Marriage Made in Heaven" be a testament to the future and hope that God has in store for you.

Book Summary: "Marriage Made in Heaven: A Christian Guide to Love"

"Marriage Made in Heaven: A Christian Guide to Love" is a comprehensive and inspirational guide that delves into the depths of a Christian marriage, exploring the principles, values, and practices that make it a sacred and lasting union. This book is a journey through 12 chapters that provide valuable insights into building and nurturing a faith-filled, loving, and enduring relationship.

The book begins by laying the foundation of a Christian marriage, emphasizing the importance of faith as the bedrock of the relationship. It highlights the divine blueprint for love and marriage, drawing parallels between the love of Christ for His Church and the love shared between spouses.

Each subsequent chapter explores a crucial aspect of a "Marriage Made in Heaven," covering topics such as effective communication, intimacy, shared goals and dreams, servanthood, forgiveness, and leaving a legacy of love and faith. It offers practical guidance on how to strengthen these elements within a marriage, drawing upon biblical wisdom and Christian teachings.

Throughout the guide, the book reinforces the significance of nurturing and sustaining love within the marriage. It underlines the dynamic nature of love, highlighting the need for continual communication, quality time together, spiritual growth, forgiveness, cherishing moments, and rekindling the flame when necessary.

The book also places a strong emphasis on the role of faith, not only as the foundation of the marriage but also as a guiding force in times of challenges and adversity. It reminds couples of the enduring love of Christ and His Church as a model for their own love story.

Furthermore, the book discusses the eternal promise of a Christian marriage, serving as a beacon of hope for a world often filled with chaos and uncertainty. It emphasizes the impact of a faith-filled love story on future generations, inspiring them to seek and nurture similar relationships.

As readers conclude their journey through the guide, they are encouraged to renew their commitment to each other and look ahead with hope, knowing that their "Marriage Made in Heaven" is a journey of endless love and faith.

In "Marriage Made in Heaven: A Christian Guide to Love," readers find a comprehensive and uplifting resource that not only provides valuable insights into building a strong Christian marriage but also offers a profound reminder of the eternal promise and hope that such a marriage represents. It is a testament to the enduring power of love and faith within the sacred union of marriage.

www.ingramcontent.com/pod-product-compliance
Lightning Source LLC
LaVergne TN
LVHW010440070526
838199LV00066B/6113